Dear Parent:
Your child's love of reading starts here!

Every child learns to read in a different way and at his or her own speed. Some go back and forth between reading levels and read favorite books again and again. Others read through each level in order. You can help your young reader improve and become more confident by encouraging his or her own interests and abilities. From books your child reads with you to the first books he or she reads alone, there are I Can Read Books for every stage of reading:

SHARED READING
Basic language, word repetition, and whimsical illustrations, ideal for sharing with your emergent reader

BEGINNING READING
Short sentences, familiar words, and simple concepts for children eager to read on their own

READING WITH HELP
Engaging stories, longer sentences, and language play for developing readers

READING ALONE
Complex plots, challenging vocabulary, and high-interest topics for the independent reader

ADVANCED READING
Short paragraphs, chapters, and exciting themes for the perfect bridge to chapter books

I Can Read Books have introduced children to the joy of reading since 1957. Featuring award-winning authors and illustrators and a fabulous cast of beloved characters, I Can Read Books set the standard for beginning readers.

A lifetime of discovery begins with the magical words **"I Can Read!"**

*Visit www.icanread.com for information
on enriching your child's reading experience.*

To Luke, always, xo
—K.G.

To my daughter,
who loves snowmen
—O.V.

I Can Read Book® is a trademark of HarperCollins Publishers.

Library of Congress Control Number: 2017938987
ISBN 978-0-06-235319-1 (hardcover) — ISBN 978-0-06-235318-4 (pbk.)

Typography by Whitney Manger

17 18 19 20 21 SCP 10 9 8 7 6 5 4 3 2 1 ❖ First Edition

DUCK, DUCK, DINOSAUR

SNOWY SURPRISE

Written by Kallie George

Illustrated by Oriol Vidal

HARPER

An Imprint of HarperCollinsPublishers

This is Feather. This is Flap.

And this is their brother, Spike.

It is winter.

Winter is full of surprises.

Today the surprise is . . .

SNOW!

"Snow is cold," says Feather.

"Cold! Cold!" says Flap.

But Spike isn't cold.

Spike wants to play.

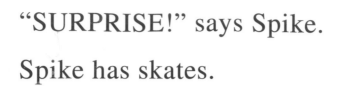

"SURPRISE!" says Spike.

Spike has skates.

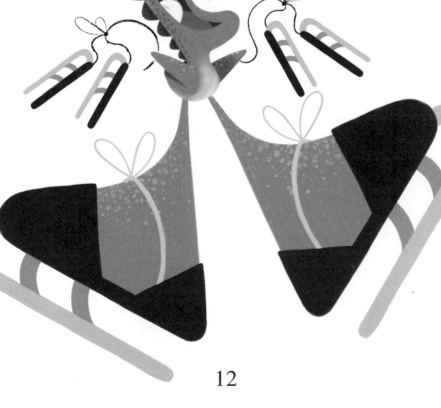

Off they go.

Off to the pond.

Whish!

Feather, Flap, and Spike skate.

"Skating is cold," says Feather.

"Too cold! Too cold!" says Flap.

But Spike isn't cold.

Spike still wants to play.

"SURPRISE!" says Spike.

Spike has a sled.

Up they go. Up the hill.

Whoosh!

Feather, Flap, and Spike sled.

"Sledding is cold," says Feather.

"T-too c-cold! T-too c-cold!" says Flap.

But Spike isn't cold.

Spike STILL wants to play.

"SURPRISE!" says Spike.

Spike rolls a snowball.

He is ready to make a snowman.

But Feather and Flap are shaking.

Feather and Flap are shivering.

They are too cold to play.

What can Spike do?

23

"SURPRISE!" says Spike again.

Spike has mittens.

Spike has scarves.

Spike has hats.

Feather and Flap put them on.

"Winter is cold," says Feather.

"But we are warm."

"Warm! Warm!" says Flap.

Now they all want to play.

And look!

Mama brings hot cocoa.

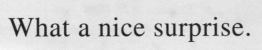

What a nice surprise.